sundaey

kirsten ihns

PROPELLER BOOKS

PORTLAND, OREGON • UNITED STATES OF AMERICA

First U.S. Edition, 2020

For further information, contact Propeller Books,
4325 Northeast Davis Street, Portland, OR 97207-1238.

Cover concept by Shawn Wheeler
Cover photo by Brett Swenson
Cover and interior design by Context

Published by Propeller Books, Portland, Oregon.
ISBN 978-0-98277-049-8

www.propellerbooks.com

contents

day day day day day day day day day day day day day day day
day day day day day day day day day day day day day day day
day day day day day day day day day day day day day day day
day day day day day day day day day day day day day day day
day day day day day day day day day day day day day day day
day day day day day day day day day day day day day day day
day day day day day sun sun sun sun sun day day day day day
day day day day day sun sun sun sun sun day day day day day
day day day day day sun sun sun sun sun day day day day day
day day day day day sun sun sun sun sun day day day day day
day day day day day sun sun sun sun sun day day day day day
day day day day day sun sun sun sun sun day day day day day
day day day day day dae dae dae dae dae day day day day day
day day day day day dae dae dae dae dae day day day day day
day day day day day dae dae dae dae dae day day day day day
day day day day day dae dae dae dae dae day day day day day
day day day day day dae dae dae dae dae day day day day day
day day day day day dae dae dae dae dae day day day day day
day day day day day dae dae dae dae dae day day day day day
day day day day day dae dae dae dae dae day day day day day
day day day day day dae dae dae dae dae day day day day day

yes, hello

i sate like sum dome creature in the sun
and i lied there, all spangled, neither truth nor hungry

      i was taken out to dance and click

obedient, i slip into Vast Amusement Model Picture

          /just appear on the screen until someone gets involved

     five times i made this thought til sweat burned on my brow
       like a razor
             bumped my sweat on the grill
         left it lonely as a sandwich
upon a crown of recollected hills, as they appear, in the literature:

       let me to beat as a pulp before you

mostly, i like things i can find by means of bathwater
behavior
lately i feel curiously free to hazard and eat them
such as: let snow show the very nature
of space to be repetition: this was all the city wanted
i.e. to be seen as drawing, or field of slowly crystallizing fluid
with a hieroglyphic punctuation, taker of first and lasting pictures
seizing its little clock in the dark, shaking it, shaking

the world of flying motor projects

i have left The Amazing Hair Day, for you
so know me
like an urgency
or a

categorization

i'm fairly unselective

i just want an order of remove

the ash on the wind is from the paper mill
and so is the smell
i blow you a kiss
and it sails the fine river of the air
very hardy
and arrives

what can i stop the breach in me
with
can i use your hair
can i use your scarf
can i use your permission

and your rarest sounds

i'm wasteful
an affordance
and the shape of a wide,
inadequate, dam

in your house i imagine you lie panting

no i don't

in your house i'm sure you turn the drapery on
as though it were responsive, or knew its states
as though they ran a legible circuit
up there
or a current

we are made with real flowers, in our prospect
                    we are a hot boat seat on the river of love
     and continuance

do you like it? i made it
          do you like it? it's of! it's of! it's of!

super fire diamond ii

every thing now
and then
surrounds bring me
back
war hair, Madonna magical
noninflection, and a play
whelk

i separate the animal from its images
into hairs
and have mercy upon them
and
speaking, addressed, and absent in my towel
i was an allergic bump between the modes
/you may call me Mister Noon
and when the microwave says what to want
i shall throw it away—

whereas his curing lamp was like
a wide bird
god was an idea of creatures
to lacerate the swamp when it sizzled and
bundled
or a lawless crawdad biscuit
hug without my smell

of the five senses, desire is the sixth

what is it to just be known

        by what you take

                    i don't see where you have a claim

are you just

      an architecture towards counting
    to rivet around its egress center
        & expensive glass

big panes
        oh i am *ready*, they say
    for my action:

i am ready to be used all the time

    /this is what the world keeps doing through me

                  heat was the great and living

          commodity

i am ready to be user all the time
& thereby

the event i fashion
sometimes it's hard to know one is

a creature
bc one feels so wholly precedent?

i think i'd like to be a complex
on the porches of my
sensation

does yours sound like this?

sometimes a formation wants
to be useless
and can't
but can't

and do so anyway

...and it's quite difficult to try

ok, rl question now

-what goes on six legs through the
costco
-and what of its species
to have no species voice nor feeling

what if i have neither species voice nor feeling

just want and the present
            of its emergence, which repeats

            the kind of object meant to sustain your relation to it
            i'm ready to be use all the time

being cooperational, we get our on network this   our own
                 way where i to feel
endures
         without knowledge
all the leaves to quiver
                   new aspens in spring
                   on the windy hillside

       new aspens in windy on the spring spring the hillside

dissolution

ion ion ion ion ion ion ion ion ion ion ion ion ion ion ion ion ion ion
ion ion ion ion ion ion ion ion ion ion ion ion ion ion ion ion ion ion
ion ion ion ion ion ion ion ion ion ion ion ion ion ion ion ion ion ion
ion ion ion ion ion ion ion ion ion ion ion ion ion ion objection ion ion
ion ion ion ion ion object object object objection ion ion ion ion ion
ion ion ion ion ion object object object objection ion ion ion ion ion
ion ion ion ion ion object object object objection ion ion ion ion ion
ion ion ion ion ion object object object objection ion ion ion ion ion
ion ion ion ion ion object object object objection ion ion ion ion ion
ion ion ion ion ion object object object objection ion ion ion ion ion
ion ion ion ion ion object object object objection ion ion ion ion ion
ion ion ion ion ion object object object objection ion ion ion ion ion
ion ion ion ion ion object object object objection ion ion ion ion ion
ion ion ion ion ion object object object objection ion ion ion ion ion
ion ion ion ion ion ion ion ion ion ion ion ion ion ion ion ion ion
ion ion ion ion ion ion ion ion ion ion ion ion ion ion ion ion ion
ion ion ion object objection ion ion ion ion ion ion ion ion ion ion ion
ion ion ion ion ion object object object objection ion ion ion ion ion ion
ion ion ion ion ion ion ion ion ion ion ion ion ion ion ion ion ion
ion ion ion ion ion ion ion ion ion ion ion ion ion ion ion ion ion
ion ion objection ion ion ion ion ion ion ion ion ion ion ion ion ion ion
ion ion ion ion ion ion ion ion ion ion ion ion ion ion ion ion ion
ion ion ion ion ion ion ion ion ion ion ion ion ion ion ion ion ion
ion ion ion ion ion ion ion ion ion ion ion ion ion ion ion ion ion

cicatrixx

tissue that has a form for its history

specific past its species

scar is a knowing a creature cannot tell

its species

to be a thing whose beginnings could be numbered

lol wat

i was staying awake in my hair cut

rode the ship around the story for the ship

like that we were together for a while

the city has moved since i was born in it

city not a fixture, this surprise

it does not matter what you bring to bear on it

it cannot be dissolved, that's to say

it can be classified as a sense of motion

it ran in a ring about where it was stapled to the knowable

to make part of it

a way that could be relied upon

that is, believed to be unchanging

or to change beside the one relying

be slow fixing

be over

and over again:

but still standing where we left it

i said i would wait but discovered i had no intentions of any kind

this encounter was brief, or discovery

like, i do as i said or i did otherwise

i am wondering all the time: *what i can really see of someone's house?*

a terrible fizz

i come to you across a revision distance

:this that accounts

i certainly am not keeping in my track

:get out and out

the kind of pleasure you can gnaw and not diminish

knot and know diminished

when its regions grow back healed

the pleasure heals from where you took it, anyway

point from which the growth comes back

the states i have been completely at?

the kind that take prepositions

in motion at work at rest in health in sick at sick

i left them in a rapid car

how long has your motion been in place

and what have you lately done about it

while the living is

been in place while the living is

my long lasted a time and then it didn't

stopped it stopped

whatever has a short during

i put the acts in their sweet cusps

under the chin they reflect

the incident light

as though wet or potential but actually neither

but still it was steam and rather nice in here

prom queen/big leaf

of the instrument, let's make it sob

       the season was in its world
             magnificent on the wet steps
       it was walking slowly down:

            the big deal of it, it was walking down, it was
      was attending to, of the gown, the hem
       & getting soaked
      and something
intruding on the aperture

the water looked like sound going fast enough
            very splashy, big as foam, as exclamation

      rocking in its dirty subjacence

         static and fireflies
      the sea was cellophane, tonight
         you live
             with the object
differently after you've made it
      carry the shape of something else
you were   it was
struggling to originate, and
     all i knew
                  i was happy to know
      in the middle of such serious music

one time is no time

time time time time time time time time time time time time time
time time time time time time time time time time time time time
time time time time time time time time time time time time time
time time time time time time time time time time time time time
time time time time time time time time time time time time time
time time time time time time time time time time time time time
time time time time time time time time time time time time time
time time time time time time time time one time time time time
time time time time time time time time time time time time time
time time time time time time time time time time time time time
time time time time time time time time time time time time time
time time time time time time time time time time time time time
time time time time time time time time time time time time time
time time time time time time time time time time time time time
time time time time time time time time time time time time time
time time time time time time time time time time time time time
time time time time time time time time time time time time
time time time time time time time time time time time time time
time time time time time time time time time time time time time
time time time time time time time time time time time time time
time time time time time time time time time is time time time
time time time time time time time time time time time time time
time time time time time time time time time time time time time
time time time time time time time time time time time time time
time time time time time time time time time time time time time
time time time time time time time time time time time time time
time time time time time time time time time time time time time
time time time time time time time time time time time time time
time time time time no time time time time time time time time
time time time time time time time time time time time time time
time time time time time time time time time time time time time
time time time time time time time time time time time time time
time time time time time time time time time time time time time
time time time time time time time time time time time time time
time time time time time time time time time time time time time
time time time time time time time time time time time time time
time time time time time time time time time time time time time
time time time time time time time time time time time time time
time time time time time time time time time time time time time

does this building tell you nicely how to enter?

i put someone else's napkins in my cup

before i leave

some constructions
some soft architecture

gusseted basal planes

meant to drop
be stitched up

achieved beyond the target
brittle forest
forest of describing vectors

foramen of the sea star
femur
repeating the near-sleep arrival vision
animal vision
animadversion

untutor   tactile vital   stellate
spread to encompass its curved disc face

even a thing wildly used

go home & eat my grapefruit

beautiful as categories, a congress
across them

hard to know

where to put my belonging

belongs to

my   female   its ness
puts the shoes on the hands
and walks   like hooves

i'm delightful
afraid of her

i sing the body
quadrupedic

       sing my walk beside it

              i sing quat swan
     i sing hat check

sing trick and deck

                              in german
       the word electrical outlet

steckdose

                shteck doza
           bulldozer

appropriate:

dozer pro equipment love

the vessel rotates in the sound goes streaming through it

-*how do you feel*
- i feel inhabited
     by my animating   concerns

how do you feel
-files and files   i feel orderly
  safety in my red hat   and oh my god *so* visible
    i feel i people this field of vision
        stick it to the image center

like: specular erotics of construction…culture
    the kind i can freely lounge inside of
    kick my feet in   feel so soundless

                      i mean, like, *no* noise
              hot & diagonal
                    at all

limitedness of view is a perfect cause

straight from   *some troubles, living in the plenum*

actually, objects   are always in a concrete situation

(lol)   *in which we continue the joke*

out of all parameters

-mixed, poured, set-

outlived

and

         spilled

its shadows freely about it

         hard to know where to put the belonging

                              you live with the object
                    differently, after you've made it
                  carry the shape of something else

                    well go on, who
          did you think was in this knock-knock

the kind of light the sound can't leave

dear ms. dozer

      it is with bashful heart that i write this
      but i felt you tremble when i stood in your shade
in your   *ventilated lifting cavern*
           slats the sky comes pouring through
   ace ace   *baby*   *blue*

dear scientific operator,

you are

dear scientific operator, set on by the event
        and a casual increase,
let me know you in your meanest contour

    and where do you lie open
        in my entered discipline
    and its bad uses

   i run my history round the yard
      it's short
          & needs an exercise

dear ms. dozer,

   my heart is

is an all night
   spot, knowing its verdict
      the true thing it could say
  by being
in the sight of others

being other people see it

     i think i mean

or maybe this

i can't ever be in the land
      scape
      can only go with my sight
      i wanted to feel bodily and in the land
            not somehow beside it
    walking like i usually do

it is like a terrarium, usually
        i encounter it like a perimeter
    i bang on the glass and scare the fish
                so they tell me to   sit down
                in the dentist's office
                              i do

      it's like that, me and where i am
              it won't let me out of the waiting room—

                  though it is also the kind of place you can't
            stay in
      like the morning
      or any hour
        range of hours

dear ms. dozer,

let me be more straightforward

describe some favorite features of the beloved

      tiny chair in your blue glass mind
      cherry
            on-a-stick-ness   of your impulse
    chirpy lemon   of your fins, yes

dear scientific operator,

      this model comes equipped
      with lights   they run on a separate electrical loop
      we find them to be reliable.

dear ms. dozer

      i have fancied the darkness of your hidden body
      the one that talks to the dirt
      so quietly
      at nite
      like a sky
      whispers some promises rushing above it

      o the darkness of your sky could fill up my night

i want you to know i envy
      every single thing you have

                            uh, destroy. destroyed

dear scientific operator,

i would propose the following alternate orthography:
deet roi

...if that's okay, i mean?

dear ms. dozer,

i envy every thing you have

deet roi

22

dear deet roi,
let's take a photo

...ok

it might help

    do we want to
        stiffen up   *do this riffing positional*   *slice*
myself on that sleepless axis

    nah   *refuse* *accession to a pleasure* stay
        with the rending   unmake   practice

        but let me
    but let me
subject you
      to a virtue
    /attention

/explain to me what love feels to you?

i think it is an intensity of the gaze
i think it is you make my breakfast
i think it is you hear
    no name but mine
    in the collected hallways of your mind
(i rly think all this ought to rhyme?)
i think it's a deflected habitual
    /more waves in fewer moments
    refresh yr wounds with salt and lime
    do that pleasure all the time

i think it's only vaguely relational
i think it's a dream in a hallway of mirrors
i think the tennis ball got lodged in the drain
/it stays late
/ stays to take
    something of the night's stark quality
        to be an excellent   *bear witness*

    how many parts   can depart *and leave* their unity
    the whole thing dies   each day *but gets up again*
    back in   *not surpassing*

    we request you please give a detailed description
  of your perception   of time passing

i'd like an affection to take me past myself
spend my life
to forge the bridge to take me over

.......i think it's actually more like a total inadequacy of the municipal
storm sewer   system?

i think is *you*
make my breakfast
where a heat outside my thinking
knocks to get in

(some specifications re breakfast):

jam
meyer lemons
the nice kind of paper napkin
resumption of no body
right here

i want my ~~sanctioned~~ sectioned fruit and a videotape of my
  pleasure arriving
seamlessly

i take my apples sliced   nonviolently

make them a new shape
knowing capacity for want

make them hungry or not

but then the morning went on and stayed on as long as i watched it
  nice
as a vegetal rhythm   nixed in it   making
suitable frolic   fickle   tilled   waxed   shameless
like
it is summer   whose quantity of mundane light

permits modalities made like
do you like

to know the fact of x place

        i don't know information very well

        know with the wrong organ

        conflate myself with my receiving

        /i don't get up from what i see

wall wall wall wall wall wall wall wall wall wall wall wall wall wall
wall wall wall wall wall wall wall wall wall wall wall wall wall wall
wall wall wall wall wall wall wall wall wall wall wall wall wall wall
wall wall wall wall wall wall wall wall wall wall wall wall wall wall
wall wall wall wall wall wall wall wall wall wall wall wall wall wall
wall wall wall wall wall wall wall wall wall wall wall wall wall wall
wall wall wall wall wall wall wall wall wall wall wall wall wall wall
wall wall wall wall wall wall wall wall wall wall wall wall wall wall
wall wall wall wall wall wall wall wall wall wall wall wall wall wall
wall wall wall wall wall wall wall wall wall wall wall wall wall wall
wall wall wall wall wall wall wall wall wall wall wall wall wall wall
wall wall wall wall wall wall wall wall wall wall wall wall wall wall
wall wall wall wall wall wall wall wall wall wall wall wall wall wall
wall wall wall wall wall wall wall as though she wasn't sure wall w
wall wall wall wall wall wall wall wall where her stomach was wall
wall wall wall wall wall wall wall wall wall wall wall wall wall wall
wall wall wall wall wall wall wall wall wall wall wall wall wall wall
wall wall wall wall her yellow coat looks very thick and soft wall w
wall wall wall wall like what you'd imagine folded inside a wall wa
wall wall wall wall wall wall wall wall wall wall wall wall wall wall
wall wall wall wall wall wall wall wall wall wall wall wall wall wall
wall wall wall wall wall wall wall wall wall wall wall wall wall wall
wall wall wall wall wall wall wall wall wall wall wall wall wall wall
wall wall wall wall wall wall wall wall wall wall wall wall wall wall
wall wall wall wall wall wall wall wall wall wall wall wall wall wall

very thick and soft

wall wall wall wall wall wall wall wall wall wall wall wall wall wall
wall wall wall wall wall wall wall wall wall wall wall wall wall wall
wall wall wall wall wall wall wall wall wall wall wall wall wall wall
wall wall wall wall wall wall wall wall wall wall wall wall wall wall
wall wall wall wall wall wall wall wall wall wall wall wall wall wall
wall wall wall wall wall wall wall wall wall wall wall wall wall wall
wall wall wall wall wall wall wall wall wall wall wall wall wall wall
wall wall wall wall wall wall wall wall wall wall wall wall wall wall
wall wall wall wall wall wall wall wall wall wall wall wall wall wall
wall wall wall wall wall wall wall wall wall wall wall wall wall wall
wall wall wall wall wall wall wall wall wall wall wall wall wall wall

wall wall wall wall wall wall wall wall wall wall wall wall wall wall

perception is a room with the detail of walking in it
having a body is like finding
the deep end of the furniture
wanting and being nothing
to do about it

do you have a clear idea
how you want this to feel?

i mean, beforehand?

and what about a one time
one time, one time

one time face

(the moisture really is too
good

        for this

*self-portrait as horrible
smear*

/convincing self-portrait

or i just set out to limit my
environment

or i want to take my romance
with the real objects to the
next level, please

or make them arrive
   with their actions in place

in the style of a bona fide
ulterior

)

i.e. *to have the former look about it*

/how it has pleased the world to determine the matter

resume: view from the beginning arches its back

view from the beginning longs for a pet

corundum little

sap fire
                    as if to its linear thinness
            amounted five years
            a wanted to say yes
achieved
            like a choral sound, a picking
unicity off
        surfaces that catch it
                    couldn't
drag it still but tried—

            the loop treats me gently, instead

thank you for this evening
        thank you for this evening

            an intercessional kind of voice
        and that incessant chime
                    posed like /solution

        kill me in my image
        its beautiful house
        kill me with my image

            is it okay? perhaps you are wondering

    it was an easy ecstasy
after the mitochondria
            the sound the paper made seemed more important
    what it was precisely not was inaudible
a growing kind of fact
                    in the air

& rly

/

                              i like it
                    i don't want it to stop

(don't want it to stop)

no chemist

i whisper /select for me from your universe/
i pronounce it "see_lect"

my feelings for that ear are oceanic
and indecent
how else should i signify my business?
in which i mime the body like a lap
in the pool
it's perfectly as cruel as true
it's recent and it's chlorinated

i put a cleanup on the cantaloupe
       i put a needless stamp
then eat it
            while you watch?
disgusting
i answer to everyone
and can you fault me

deep sea sunday

you know i love to ask for mercy

but on the lawn, ice is not, assuredly, sea creatures

/so they tell me

i was watching you, too, though i was

        the one that was fake looking?
      that fish is called a sturgeon

daddy or nobody else

they still don't know what that noise was and it moves

activities we can do while the moon

on a clear night

over a long expanse of lawn

shines. the monster squid
from #4 can be a colossal squid
because it was much bigger
than a giant squid or

sunbeams, what if i don't get to talk to you

      in all this good lighting

   we have?

      and in what body would you keep it? let it out
    snap its leash, lay my fine life at its regular feet

always Photo Shop their photos when it includes the hugest animals

on this topic meanwhile, i'll tell you, what do sunfish taste like?

can i order it to eat it?
can i order it to eat naturally?
can i order it to eat any object?

number three looks like a Stur Gene, photo shopped, i think

it was to include huge animals, that we did it

meant no harm to any creature, any fancy vision

she communicated extremely clearly: "let us go out then, and dance"

i invite the lightning in, i make it tea

and who would leave such a splendid chance? i'm for scientific
   options
and the splendor of a wicked tune

snapped over the lined-up

no, it was merely some kind of stride you were

walking through

Hackchetfish are found in Finding Nemo

Penguins aren't sea creatures, they're birds!

i like how you sound

so enthusiastic

but why can't anyone

hold their camera steady?

i went to the man who was in charge
and found him like a sordid conclusion

you don't have to develop your photo shop in
the dark

any more

i said, removing the pins around the door

speaking very slowly

    why are octopuses goo, at war

i said and dropped the last and wait

in the sudden light i couldn't see his face

    are you doing just fine?

    i could have fired this water

    clear across the dry

rattling sound the sun would make as it streamed

i swear a whole sunbeam in my eye

's the only thing that stopped me

    you're a liar, said the man in charge
    almost like a person does,
    walking his stride through the whole damned door
    on the leash i had snapped and left on the
    grass

    we were outside, after all

bap tart powerglide

the shape receives its alien guests—honors and devours them
  /hold still, i like to be generous

    then i get that
/immobility of a sentiment which has swallowed whole rabbits/
      i see farther is a thing from you

      i see your salivary power glide
          do some donuts
                in the donut shop
                          parking lot
      /hot

          i think *let me live like a terrible thing all year*
              a swarm of little inconsistent objects,
                  passing on the stage
        as the stage
              then off

    /would you feel me in your chest
clatter down your labored respiration
        i reproduce by kind permission

                    and can i place you in this ghost
          let you fur me very feely
              touch expensive for no reason
                  splashing in the neon
                      dream of satin sheets
                      and peanut
              butter toast—
                          it comes again
        i like to draw it out
              in the object matter of relation
                    leaf matter
              litter, let's take it slow
          where even the showboat climbs your household

sundaey

live footage of the mimic octopus
        gently will i grab its neck
                      and twist
        the footage

nobody suspects a thing

                i said i was not to swim
        out that far, the sea being full
    of nope
        and sightings

surely with the proper slope would i bear up
        but my slope is very, is sleek, improper
  and i'm so given to release—

    can one discharge this symptom
        honorably
  can one discharge it in
    a crowd
             /let me clean my dirty teeth
      the old cat twitches in his sleep

    the drab garb of my utmost
shock technician
      rattles dryly in the dark

    he participates in meanings of increasing complexity
  i don't tell him how to, i just increase it
we have a rotating thing
        called The President
    and a rule
      called
         do you want me to say enough?
      we pass it back and forth

at the end, the game will ask me for
/an shelter/
  an jet
which even such plastic, freaks

precious ultra litter

mention my name when you touch me

mention your plastic strategy repertoire?

or the hypothetical imperative scenario

or the space technician

or the renewable hopscotch configuration?

i would like that.

      if you could, in parallel, say very slowly, maintaining

      my gaze, "or are you unable to

now, organize your experience"

quickly become healthy!

leave no skin in the sink!

keep the pets outside of the rain!

and brush them!

dress me in the body mesh

i spent the afternoon trying to be
a set towards the referent

&

endless uses throughout the furniture

/i wanted to be as good as an amazon review

as laid bare
      in my interjections
            like one name being used by two people

            like how vowel means /sound that permits/
      duration—

               -yeah, it was just last Thursday
               -yeah, i was like
               -it's an open field so you knew
               -it was a long time

it was everything i said it was

      when children generate their spontaneous little songs

i was outside what i meant what i said
what i meant when i said
               i had to correct that

it said very plainly that it did not wish to be subject to iteration
and i said then The Things Become Infected by the Rocket-ness
   Surrounds Them

           and it did! it went like i said

snake poem

/feel the chill of an occasion

and an atmosphere to lose my crispness
in, i find my bedroom

so beautiful, at night—a golden light the lamp is throwing
thru the folding shade

dispassionate, i rotate
i follow many snakes, the accounts are named
-daily.snakes
-daily.snakes.uk
-snake.ig
-snakes_beauty

my favorites are albino snakes

albino super motley titanium

completely worth my wait

the common krait is a venomous snake, you can find it
in the hot jungles on the south
it is of the deep subcontinent

when it bites, the coral snake can freeze
the breathing muscles

the coral snake can bite
but not through thickness
its teeth are short
and ineffective, it prefers to flee
it prefers
smaller prey

i love to watch the creatures in a cage

i love a pet i cannot hold while feeling

unafraid. i love a mind i cannot know

hi guys.. I have a huge concern. I have a few months old
Bumblebee BP .... she perches on her tree .. and spins just her head
in circles.... what may cause this?

wintergreen, canada tea
dry throat, and nostalgia
it strikes like an illness of the inner eye
and an envy to shock the material
a thin gesture
a thin and perilous gesture

would you kiss me? the doctor is in

the problem is the spider gene. it causes the head
to wobble in the BP

BP is for ball python, a popular breed
i am afraid your pet has neurologic disease
that cannot be got out
very readily? maybe other people

have some different thoughts

on this?

these videos are my personal experience

is there a fire anaconda?

does anyone have a fire anaconda?
if you could
let me know

spectra paper iris

i had not wanted to be so
                              violet
i had not wanted to be so violet
i had not wanted to be so violet
i had not wanted to be so violet
i had not wanted to be so violet
i had not wanted to be so violet
i had not wanted to be a violet
i am not wanted to be, so violet
i had not wanted to be so violet
i had not wanted to be, so violet
i had not wanted to be so violet
i had not wanted to be so violet
i had not wanted to be so violet
i am not wanted to be, so violet
i had not wanted to be so violet
i had not wanted to be so violet
i had not wanted to be a violet
i had not wanted to be so violet
i had not wanted to be so violet
i am not wanted to be, so violets
i had not wanted to be so violets
i had not wanted to be so violet
i had not wanted to be so a violet
i had not wanted to be so violet
i had not wanted to be so violet
i had not wanted to be so violet
i was not wanted to be low violet
i had not wanted to be so violet
i am not wanted to be a violet
i had not wanted to be so violet
i had not wanted to be so violet
i am not wanted to be so violet
i had not wanted to be so violet
i had not wanted to be so violet
i had not wanted to be so violet
i had not wanted to be so violet
i am not wanted to be so violet
i had not wanted to be so violet
i had not wanted to be so violet

i had not wanted to be so violet
i had not wanted to be so violet
i had not wanted to be so violet
i had not wanted to be so violet
i had not wanted to be so violet
i had not wanted to be so violet
i had not wanted to be a violet
i had not wanted to be a violet
i had not wanted to be a violet
i had not

health unit

a numerous train
a triple Brass, like angels
congregant around a smooth idea
of....numbers. yep.

in this they traverse the whole cool
future
the comparator tube, glass & fluky unit   flake
you'd not show up
want to look over the verge?
try this
dim mini
hap shack we can know the sign
by:
prick, the finger on it, singe it, haptic
pull the blood of a perfect sample
tuna dipstick consequences,
tennis racket drumstick
christmas   trismus
fidget wizard
nosebleed, hot boy,
stacked

stacked
stacked

watch for
-play mai little weapon on the loose, leaf shadows
-true likelihood: yard injury sustenance
-careless hour refuge under
-dash & penguins, penguin video representation, vices
-slices, as the flesh upon a copper blade

when did i know i had the tetanus?
so slow!
it was not like a hot infection

the nail went in between my toes
through my big work boot, the woofy floor

the wet and grass awareness
glass the tube they use, i see no needle
freeze in my fear i water globule? no i will not take it
to the hospital

by these signs one understands
one knows one is infected
how does one correct it?
one waits humbly in the bathroom
with tissues

and is there another way to approach the weather?
it gets between us

rapture

bird says to lime twig

      i feel our touching like a hot streak

which standpoint
insistently tropical
left a tiny furze
on my mind to things

                said the lime twig:

            i want to go in a new door
      even if it leads to the same building
as the others

full vest/terminal plush

let me insist i do not fume, the mood rode in
on several horses
while my dress was actually

...and i found i couldn't stop it

it scared the life out at me, my own
blast off, i pressed the button

:an event dedicated to its non-specificity
or /how would *you* describe it

let me have it
ok, i let you have it

my mother said i was dis-tempered
but i refuse to answer my description
when it comes for me
and is reliable

it even offers to transform my water
and *still* i tell it no(!)

....then it hangs around the doors for a while

there was a time i could not understand
and also one in which i could not understand the fuss
just learned its terms
to repeat them exactly
in the style of a mastered language

:how would you describe it?
it smelled extremely
you fluoresce thru it

when did you become
described & did it hurt you

creature not let out of its countenance
/yard with a fence
this was like no other machine i have ever had
at various and calculated speeds
it advises
be a form of vast comportment
example: Pat likes to fill the tub
example: the flood is kept in orderly current

i want to do the exactness of my work
gray, waxed, super, fine

at all points permit the ornament to wash
up on the shores of a real decorum

but too much sail
said /trim your sails/ and i didn't do it
but i thought
is this life the entire time

violet plant

violate violate
violate violate
violate violate
violate violate

foliate foliate foliate
foliate foliate foliate
foliate foliate foliate
foliate foliate foliate
foliate foliate foliate
foliate foliate foliate
foliate foliate foliate
foliate foliate foliate
foliate foliate foliate
foiliate foliate foliate
foliate foliate foliate
foliate foliate foliate
foliate foliate foliate
foliate foliate foliate
foliate foliate foliate
foliate foliate foliate
foliate foliate foliate

quat swan

anchored in the steep water
tendered in its sunset color
vectored in a dive descriptor

the lines begin the same but then they aren't

they tend to
they lose their anchor
and they are
there is the spray!

they are there
phare   thy eye is where it tends

i said, enunciating very clearly,

     "xx me like a swan"

     as though this were charming
     or demonstrated my practicality

i want very much to demonstrate

home: this is not a reference to leda in the swan
stop reading that in right now
exactly now

do it now do now

do it now

now?

now do it

i wonder if love necessitates
                    a complexity of attention
        cooperativity   (captivity?)

quat swan   quat the swan: "aquatic aquatic"

                stop thinking about leda

quat and did you

                                        quat the swan:

glacier

...and it was meant to be a joke

flotation device   even the hyper imperator

can't tell
the value of a thing   in terms of itself

example: the day passes by
recording its numerals

example: this is not a thought

example: a thought you could put in your mind
to make it two

in order to make it to

or what else do i do everything for

quat the swan:

stack   drastic as its ending cause
i wish to enter the gift economy
gluttony gluttony

i wish wish plush
i wish wish do

                        /let no one say i hesitate

/i wish i do

dayglow circular   lap devices

a thing that wants to flee its center
              or enter it

enter it quat the swan

it quat it quat

i mean do me

i mean with me

i know the song they are playing
it is lucky to be born in the morning

                                    sit up straight in your night location
i want to turn the face of the god   stuck in its infinite number existence?

she said quat

                    said quat swan

                    no more hat check, hat trick
                    deck deck

                    no more than three people in this

                    this is a platform at a time

when it crashes they will sort the remnants
you don't need to worry about that   is an non in-advance trouble

the man says he gave his
daughter a name that means
          a rain of gold
     a like a name a hold a significance

/this the simplicity of its facts

                    you cannot contain the gold, it gets out
          and ruins things
                    in a wax even pet cleaner cannot remove

for you, for you

quat the swan

go on up and comfort the miracle

she pushes me forward with   this is encouragement

here is a space meant to house the event
a room that could fit an emergency in it

sometimes i am afraid to stop eating
sometimes i am afraid to stop eating

sometimes i am afraid that if i do

it will be if i do

a room that could fit an emergency in it

house the event

i don't ask much

the kind of scene you can be   all   in

lacks no daisies, that one

                              in the gold we find a dilute
presence of the sun of god
/if enough gold is there
                    it is light in here

that's the going theory

kumquat

orange

                                   identifying its variables
                         the fiber was pleasingly masticated
                    we put it outside to dry

but then it was eaten and could not be turned into rope

so it is that the group is learning
i do not know these enemy
that my mind own lives in
(own mind lives in?)
miscible   and then finally
tonic

                                        aquatic big swam

                              what id it today
i did today

that's okay, this kind of thing can be done like the mouth is

                    pleather pleather pleather

quat the swan:

        let me give you an object that refuses to close
                        around its area of rest

quat the swan:

an almost nothing decoration

and there it was

the demiurge was in the language like a transitive verb

that's why i love her so much. i mean english [in response to some
   confusion]

i think i am quoting from davie here but
maybe not exactly quoting

maybe some word like quote

?

::tangerine

mandarin among them
martinet
my whip n my furs

marten pine marten deprived thereof

so maybe we don't do that

in the firs in its black eyes globose like a morula

       tender

quat the swan, remembering with fondness

         quat the swan she likes to stroke

all the thefts that never leave
just sitting there
on the lawn

like geese

i began to love u when you failed to respond to my will

duck duck goose u became the world
& cut the glass across its reflex
u were fast
& did not sink into the lake

/were as sudsed as a surfactant doing lifting
and a holographic pleasure was the kind that yours would be
like the vermilion-flinging sequins of Renée Fleming
's operatic pink champagnely dress—

like feathers ripping from the sofa
a sun that plunges down into the TV

refraction indices

want to do that thing where i repeat
    the perception
the water is
        a hungry glass
i catch
      my mother looking in me
          arranging her hair

the equipment era dawns like this

the kind of song where the singer wears
their heart on their sleeve

    then does away with it
            in spectacular fashion

    and that's the end!   we think! but then!

she winks and calls it up and says

      i missed you

    when i shot the other troubles

and there's a pause
      in which exactly
no one laughs
    in this stadium-style banana can, it's flat
fizzless, not even
  our woman on the stage is acting like she gets it

it bangs its knees, stumbling around in the orchestra pit
    breaks the spirit of the best violin
      the one whose role had been to say

we dream like twins in paradise

we dream like twins in paradise

warm occasion

in all my limbs i zittern

in all my limbs i refuge like my body is adornment

oh from what is merely not
i draw my one pony
my trick:
-the doormat
-the /to each creature its affordance/
on the porch of its
inundation
i bring each question fumbling to your shore
and constellated
with elaborate jewels
they come in like the world
/delicto, uncertain, stopless, asking
in whose image have you
deformed the material
i make
a shush gesture
i proliferate
the silence signs
but the herd disperses at your
touch

it does

it always

after josef albers

```
read   read   read   read   read   read   read   read   read
read   read   read   read   read   read   read   read   read
read   read   read   read   read   read   read   read   read
read   read   read   read   read   read   read   read   read
read   read   read   read   read   read   read   read   read
read   read   read   read   read   read   read   read   read
read   read   read   read   read   read   read   read   read
read   read   read   read   read   read   read   read   read
read   read   read   read   read   read   read   read   read
read   read   read   read   read   read   read   read   read
read   read   read   green  green  green  read   read   read
read   read   read   green  green  green  read   read   read
read   read   read   green  green  green  read   read   read
read   read   read   green  green  green  read   read   read
read   read   read   green  green  green  read   read   read
read   read   read   green  green  green  read   read   read
read   read   read   green  green  green  read   read   read
```

```
yellow yellow yellow yellow yellow yellow yellow yellow yellow
yellow yellow yellow yellow yellow yellow yellow yellow yellow
yellow yellow yellow yellow yellow yellow yellow yellow yellow
yellow yellow yellow yellow yellow yellow yellow yellow yellow
yellow yellow yellow yellow yellow yellow yellow yellow yellow
yellow yellow yellow yellow yellow yellow yellow yellow yellow
yellow yellow yellow yellow yellow yellow yellow yellow yellow
yellow yellow yellow yellow yellow yellow yellow yellow yellow
yellow yellow yellow yellow yellow yellow yellow yellow yellow
yellow yellow yellow yellow yellow yellow yellow yellow yellow
yellow yellow yellow yellow yellow yellow yellow yellow yellow
yellow yellow yellow violent violent violent yellow yellow yellow
yellow yellow yellow violent violent violent yellow yellow yellow
yellow yellow yellow violent violent violent yellow yellow yellow
yellow yellow yellow violent violent violent yellow yellow yellow
yellow yellow yellow violent violent violent yellow yellow yellow
yellow yellow yellow violent violent violent yellow yellow yellow
yellow yellow yellow violent violent violent yellow yellow yellow
yellow yellow yellow violent violent violent yellow yellow yellow
yellow yellow yellow violent violent violent yellow yellow yellow
yellow yellow yellow violent violent violent yellow yellow yellow
yellow yellow yellow violent violent violent yellow yellow yellow
```

lay the fine life on a muster of rocks

they sang a requiem at the beginning of the universe
    i'll spend all of my time as soon as i get it

a recalculated piñata
    you can know it
              by the virtuosity of the cleanness
     below it

what is the source of light in this painting
    -the police

the thing that struck me always is

what is the source of light in this pantry
    an interruption of money
    it then settles me
    to sit in a style apparently whole

    hi i'm here in particular for disclosure
      and miraculous knitwear
         does it make you feel weird?
        i can't stop the rain

an info to cherish

                              a lot of it

collected what fell on the ground

just as a puzzle

                    seven thousand people are watching it now

          for in it miraculous, by only and things

the region grew so lately fatal

          coming up cruxes, coming up spring, the sign

          conquers by signs, the tulip bulbs and daffodils

          yes, but where is it that you work

          to watch and grow

          a scent in the air, utter and ordinary,

          i developed an expanded box of senses

          sense of the type, the beauty, function

          of hearing bent to other purpose, dim

          what is the pan, be taken thus

          at minimal angles

          absolute extremely harm is pretty

          aweful and surprising as it breaks across the screen

          imagine your neighbor naked and mowing

          i use the hottest water

for this i live with the ambulances passing by

buying an infinite pen, & a fringe of Georgia window

good luck for all French bread, they say

calm and slicing. wat if sun is risne

rinse, phenomenal addition

nominal math and math

        can in new pleasure
where i will star with another person
day, or trying to improve

that until everyone die, amazing music
it is nice to meet ppl
meanwhile, some girl is wasting paper
i detach the elasticated waist of my underwear
band
glitching stream
froot loop
organic fruit delivered to your door
the spoor of wild creatures cast upon the heath
the first time i have seen an ass in traces
a video you can edit again and again
approaching no nearer edge
are you a faith person's
princely hologram
tide knocked knees
he said prepare the waiter cress i said ok
i did an experimentation with the wall paper
i said we can make it like a screen print contact paper
keeping everything totally angry
sanitary
since how long is this continuous
for a car the color silver is least good
i like a favorite subject
i was just curious if there was anyone else out there
you scare, despite your fearless head and sour cream
jam is in a cup
you set me free
there was no school i wanted to do

the sky is a dark wonderful dark
outside the room is where do you stay at
i have been listening for hours, you aren't
returning
see you in the hell my dear
you have a nice set
you have a nice set up
i made the wall into part of myself
i am not from texas
oooh, sleigh bells
is this emilie
what is it called
hello is this emilie
i drink water and sleep
dream about, a plant to become
/person walking endless in a circle
 incarnate under sunlight
                    red
in fact it is a need that produces a time
                to walk beneath
                        to walk thru carnations
and bear the site of their event
i lay me down for the tenderness of ankles
the sounds are difficult to place
they come so quickly to my ears
but stay? for ever and ever on right
it expands
i look for chilled people in the chat
like a scrap, i swim up to the surface
the light was green and very reflective, and i was
...i liked it

rly i like the music's modern kick
in practical singing flies the cage apart
the universe is a garage
garbage
rag and gelid shrieks it past
hi
i dislike slosh
to fill the guts you change it very rapidly
order and concentric,
all my evidence you must have been
a fine reference y'all just chill

stop to secure the cargo
belts and belt loops, we're a couple
love and lay my
idek if you remember
reamer, slicer paper pepperoni andino
my biological grade is a b
not even a plus
that's....so kind
these legs are so long
she has offered to help me make my surfaces
are you sure you don't have a crush on her?
it sounds like y'all are interacting a lot
of the chex mix, let me know if i can be more helpful
clair de lung, yr kind of an expert
at this point

tightly

wound wound wound wound wound wound wound wound wound
wound wound wound wound wound wound wound wound wound
wound wound wound wound wound wound wound wound wound
wound wound wound wound wound wound wound wound wound
wound wound wound wound wound wound wound wound wound
wound wound wound wound wound wound wound wound wound
wound wound wound wound wound wound wound wound wound
wound wound wound wound wound wound wound wound wound
wound wound wound wound wound wound wound wound wound
wound wound wound wound wound wound wound wound wound
wound wound wound wound wound wound   wound wound
wound wound wound wound wound wound   wound wound
wound wound wound wound wound wound   wound wound
wound wound wound wound wound wound   wound wound
wound wound wound wound wound wound   wound wound
wound wound wound wound wound wound   wound wound
wound wound wound wound wound wound   wound wound
wound wound wound wound wound wound   wound wound
wound wound wound wound wound wound   wound wound
wound wound wound wound wound wound   wound wound
wound wound wound wound wound wound   wound wound
wound wound wound wound wound wound wound wound wound
wound wound wound wound wound wound wound wound wound
wound wound wound wound wound wound wound wound wound
wound wound wound wound wound wound wound wound wound
wound wound wound wound wound wound wound wound wound

military blimp

fix it how you like it   such a loophole   then dinner

i live in an area
i live at two distance

        i'm thrilled to be here, really thrilled
            i do not even need to manage my respiration

        it was an atmosphere was a mute day, misty, made one
            think of the hard durable products of empire
                but then the calendar was so soft   to me

            this is a late 90s representation
        it hovers near the neural net, the allium, the realized supernova
                now they get online in the forest

        now think about bitcoin mining
                in Venezuela
                    like a tourist

of the massive accounting ambition
                it is obviously volcanic
                    it is not obviously fluffy
            he is hereby anointed with an asterisk, verily
                        and changed

            life is metabolism and irritable
        is soak the scenery
                        too much
        thus the weather came up like a window
                    of opportunity
            then came about like a commentary
                    then jesus stopped and started it

        and the lawnmower razed the grass

now, take this ballistic quiz
                and this miracle from the sky
        and everything i have to give you

lay it gently in your soft deep burden
lay it in the seat of some thoughts
that furnish that /situation/ kind of look

we can't make images of things
thinks Miranda, as she looks at the shipwreck

and sometimes it can be wished that the weather would
not even show up

remember, infrastructure has needs
and glamorous maintenance

as it makes its precursors from the really unlikely
material it makes them from
like unrelated paintings
like, in the war department, we are thinking
about a humanly fabricated sort of cloud
in a humanly fabricated cloud
it is not banal
it is not stupid

it is not very stupid
it is a baby thing, now
and was a lemon of abounding

move through it on a vehicle

i went through a vehicle
then a phase, then i enjoyed the food, the god, control
i scraped the metal facings on the wall

i moved from a bird's eye point
to i used the foot
as the composing instrument
the spray toilette
footstep function means is used by people
and the Chinese opera of the empty stage
gingerly was i thinking
i was movements
arising in my one unwary body
as the actor is a walker onstage

for example, they are walking through a door
for example, the door is formed by their movement
for example in such a way may an entered door be

completed

conjured with implements
and closed
but by what compass
may the soul come thereby in
quite wholly—

these roofs are red so the drones may know
who to spare

the movement of danger is when
you value it
would you come false to my hand, you ask it

quietly, the states sing their state songs
in the dry sage brush, dry insects make
their noises to each other
there is nothing particularly for you here

but do please do come

user, satisfacer

con con con con con con con con con con con con con con con con con con
con con con con con con con con con con con con con con con con con con
con con con con con con con con con con con con con con con con con con
con con con con con con con con con con con con con con con con con con
con con con con con con con con con con con con con con con con con con
con con con con con con con con con con con con con con con con con con
con con con con content tent tent tent tent tent tent content con con con
con con con con content tent tent tent tent tent tent content con con con
con con con con content tent tent tent tent tent tent content con con con
con con con con content tent tent tent tent tent tent content con con con
con con con con content tent tent tent tent tent tent content con con con
con con con con content tent tent tent tent tent tent content con con con
con con con con content tent tent tent tent tent tent content con con con
con con con con content tent tent tent tent tent tent content con con con
con con con con content tent tent tent tent tent tent content con con con
con con con con content tent tent tent tent tent tent content con con con
con con con con content tent tent tent tent tent tent content con con con
con con con con content tent tent tent tent tent tent content con con con
con con con con con con con con con con con con con con con con con con
con con con con con con con con con con con con con con con con con con
con con con con con con con con con con con con con con con con con con

flexile, textile, and delight/(textile change operator/operator/orderly cream)

                              know the hinge of your inclination

                    wrack it out
           wrap it around
                    the set up the video
     original, all of this is original
                    of a cloud: driven before the wind

           does yours sound like that

throwing the look of a solid area
era

           know the fences of it
                              by encounter
     know them w elastic gladness

/wrap o.s. around them

yea tho the hours would unyoke me

from me
        have me
                be instant

i wanted to be

        a diachronic kind of picture

            i repeat my hinges
                        hinges

        tell me more facts?
    born up and raised
in the big yard
                of expectations, i'm just waiting for my display

            :it smelled like lunch in the inside room
        & i had only the other idea about it:

        knowing how to use the door
                                for instance

i want to believe i am
the shapes i make with my life

        it didn't seem to have "sprung" or to have come
from anywhere but its suddenness
                and its suddenness
                        was in there like a quality

&

what is   *i have ?*

just out here sieving peas
        cork voice going out on the nice
    the night   is peace
            is flash
            is me
                    is lash
                    refresh
                        it does
                        it lash and lasts
i regret
regress
refresh the page

                            cork voice going out on the night-
        saturated sail   in the dark to have arrived
            before the candles
        chandelle, mortadella, amanita, xx was *huge*
tige de suif we stuck it out   we lit the room we flash
                            we flash
                            we very nice refresh
                                the page

        we lash we do!
                        we   through and through
        i was trying for the we, you write, you're right
                        like that
                you read me right like that
    too red me in my room
sundayed pastry costume
        sun clayed
                to be so fresh you get a cold
        walls sleek cornure, untorsioned
/that's the dream
                    that hatch, dirt cordant
                        /it ripped the sound in two

                        i was
                into it
                it was a toss-up
                it really was

                    perfectly as good
          as easter green
     slick as grace
               as grass
                  cold supple
                         frischer coffee
               task! task-task
                    but...i *like* some structure in my task!

          under the blows of the whip of pleasure   wipe
                    foo-*weh!* foo-wet!
          :to hear the thwack

o to hear it in my very skin
          i hear it in the easter grass
     they zigzag leave the bow rubans!
   the note out here, it gets so flat
AND THE SCREEN GOT SUDDENLY ENGLISH
          :screen god sudden act

          ...then my life did that thing i like with its eyes

          a thing

          any thing

                              -you drew down night?
                         -yeah, i drew down night

                              /i refresh the ice
                                refresh my nice

                         we did it to me very casualty

-can you tell me the name of the distance
between any thing identical with itself

-delight

becomes pictorial
when viewed through pain

so they say

sooth, they say

where it tends

/they are there. phare
        thy eye is where it tends:

                          i looked around and all
                            i could see
                  was partitioning

            /i looked around and could not see that
              all i could see
        was partitioning
                  but felt i knew it?

/know your fences like a sweetness

run up against them

again

/the love is in the iteration

/the heart becomes engorged
        & wraps around the fence
           the heart becomes

    trying for the we, you write

                  & would make a little drawing there

where the body senses
by changing
      itself

for hours
in the storm are there then no objects out the
window
then suddenly can one not remove the window
from the sight
what sight the spirit has
/just snow

to perceive is to take for true, says one who sets out
to take the shirt of the world
& not put it on, to just remove it

& would make a little drawing there too

...when there is not finally plus light

the illumination is not to be borne

it lets itself go in the poetry

splashing in its four jewel eye

that's too cute

its fourth july

for july

i'm being cute

i'm being really cute

on the fourth of the july

the artifices of the fires

fell in the pool

feel in the pool and then get out

well go on
        who did you think was in this knock-knock

mouse. mouse-mouse.

      the kind of light the sound can't leave

it is getting meanwhile
very late in here

it is just ha. it is ha-ha.

    ok.

it, you want to know what the /it/ is

what is the it of the poems?
      nobody knows
  it was making
new consciousness
that the economy can!
for live in
& sell

dame thing
big house

        tho it really only sulks and pouts
     i sulk and pout i silk it out

  she shops for dinner at the local sprouts

my thoughts arrange it radial
my empathy it makes a square
i cut the corners
off before it sandwich, meanwhole
this was on my nicest plate
i was trying, ok
i was trying

i try and then i make it friends
i show my flag my white
decorum
i show it off my nicest lens
i try to get the outside in
but it's having none about it

things i do best: sorry and
awkward
things i do best: again

no matter how much news there is
i always want it more
i refresh the entry bin, i wipe it clean
i sanitize the gym machine before i mount
i post
i like that post
i'm posting up and down
around the ring the horse will spook
umbrella!   someone opens in the rain
and throws you off

we are with me at the twelve
years old

i bleed some minor blood
there in the expensive dust i rent
i waited for my mother
but she didn't come, she had
gone home, so i got back
on and loved the horse again—

it took me home
i took its saddle
off
and it got dark but didn't rain

notes

"after josef albers" is based on Josef Albers's "Homage to the Square" series. He says of this series in his 1964 artist statement: "Choice of the colors used, as well as their order, is aimed at an interaction — influencing and changing each other forth and back."

"one time is no time" plays briefly with the phrase "I sing the body electric" from Walt Whitman's *Leaves of Grass*.

"flexile [...]" borrows and reconfigures a pair of lines from Emily Dickinson's 572 (45): "delight becomes pictorial/when viewed through pain," and a phrase from Baudelaire's "Recueillement" [Meditation]: "Sous le fouet du Plaisir, ce bourreau sans merci" [Under the whip of pleasure, this executioner without mercy].

"military blimp" is indebted to a 2018 lecture given by John Durham Peters.

"snake poem" and "deep sea sunday" borrow a few phrases from assorted YouTube comments on videos of snakes and octopuses, respectively.

"an info to cherish" borrows a number of phrases from March and April 2018 live chat streams on YouTube account ChilledCow's "lofi hip hop radio—beats to relax/study to" feature.

"lay the fine life on a muster [...]" borrows a phrase from one of @witchbitch's Instagram captions.

acknowledgments

I am very grateful to the editors/readers/staff of these journals, where versions of some of these poems first appeared:

"yes, hello" appeared in *West Branch Wired* in 2018
"the world of flying motor projects," and "an info to cherish," appeared in *Yalobusha Review* in 2018 and 2019
"super fire diamond ii" appeared in *jubilat* in 2019
"cicatrixx" appeared in *Bone Bouquet* in 2019
"no chemist" and "move through it on a vehicle" appeared in *Black Sun Lit/Digital Vestiges* in 2019
"deep sea sunday" and "bap tart powerglide" appeared in *DREGINALD* in 2018
"sundaey" appeared on *Hyperallergic* in 2018
"prom queen/big leaf" appeared in *Sonora Review* in 2018
"military blimp" and "lay the fine life on a muster of rocks" appeared in *REALITY BEACH* in 2019
"rapture" appeared in *BOAAT* in 2016
"violet plant," "user satisfacer," and "dissolution" appeared in *La Vague* in 2019
"i began to love u when you failed to respond to my will" appeared in *Phoebe* in 2019
"flexile[..]cream" appeared in *The Stockholm Review of Literature* in 2018

And to the endlessly patient and kind friends and teachers who read versions of this manuscript or the poems in it and helped make it/them much better than they were:

Shawn Wheeler, Lisa Ihns, Jesse Ihns, Tad Ihns, Cooper Johnson, Jake Fournier, Eran Eads, Dylan Furcall, Kelly Hoffer, Gerónimo Sarmiento Cruz, Srikanth "Chicu" Reddy, Jim Galvin, Edgar Garcia, Florian Klinger, John Wilkinson, Lynn Xu, Emily Wilson, Thomas Sayers Ellis, Matt Girolami, Tim DeMay, Brett Swenson, Andrew Smyth, Benjamin Krusling, Elizabeth Willis, Emily Brown, and everyone in my workshops at Iowa 2015-2017 (esp Fall 2016 <3).

To Shawn Wheeler, Brett Swenson, and Dan DeWeese, who gave this book a cover and aesthetic I love very much.

And to the following people, for kindness, mentorship, friendship, encouragement, and/or the things you've taught me, and/or for helping me continue to believe in art/writing/learning as a good thing to try to do with one's life:

My students in the UIowa Undergraduate Poetry Workshop Spring 2017, my UChicago preceptees 2018-19, Mary Anderson, Peter O'Leary, Hilary Binda, William Pope.L, CD Wu, Tom Simmons, Ashleigh Cassemere-Stanfield, Terry Benson, Jim Bobbitt, Russell Cutts, Kelsi Vanada, Emmett Rensin, Angelina Gualdoni, Evan Wisdom-Dawson, Korey Williams, Hoa Nguyen, Roxanna Curto, Hannah Brooks-Motl, Helen Ihns, Mildred Hewes, Brian Blanchfield, Toby Altman, Duriel E. Harris, the editors at *Black Warrior Review* in 2016-17 especially Shelley Feller, Michael Dumanis and the crew at *Bennington Review*, Michael Slosek, Nicholas Nace and *Hampden-Sydney Review*, Stu Watson and *Prelude*, Izzy Casey and *The Iowa Review*, Judith Taylor & Patti Seyburn and *Pool Poetry*, Ronnie Peltier and *New Delta Review*, Connie Lu and *You Are Here* at *The Offing*, everyone at *TAGVVERK*, David Ehmcke and *Columbia Review*, *Cordite Poetry Review*, Phillip B. Williams and KMA Sullivan at *Vinyl Poetry*, David Stern, Bill Brown, Sianne Ngai, Dan Morgan, Jane Gregory, Mike Schuh & The Gray Center, David Cunning, Benjamin Morgan, Mick Tiedman, Nick Sparr, Will Menegas, August the Cat, Pepperflake the Cat, & various houseplants & apologies to anyone I've forgotten(!)

And finally, huge thanks to Propeller Books & Dan DeWeese, for believing in this project and making it happen, for typesetting these odd poems, for making this book very beautifully and thoughtfully, and to Jan Verberkmoes and Lucas Bernhardt for being truly the best and most generous/helpful editors imaginable—this book is infinitely better for their work.

KIRSTEN IHNS earned her MFA from the Iowa Writers' Workshop, where she was a Teaching-Writing Fellow. She is currently a Ph.D. student and Neubauer Presidential Fellow in English at the University of Chicago, where she studies texts that seem to want to be images, co-founded the Plexiglas series at The Gray Center for Arts & Inquiry, co-organizes UChicago's Poetry & Poetics Workshop, and works for *Chicago Review*. She is from Atlanta, Georgia.

CPSIA information can be obtained
at www.ICGtesting.com
Printed in the USA
LVHW030958240121
677333LV00001B/69